Polar Bears

Maeve T. Sisk

Gareth Stevens
Publishing

Please visit our Web site, www.garethstevens.com. For a free color catalog of all our high-quality books, call toll free 1-800-542-2595 or fax 1-877-542-2596.

Library of Congress Cataloging-in-Publication Data

Sisk, Maeve T.
 Polar bears / Maeve T. Sisk.
     p. cm. – (Animals that live in the tundra)
 Includes index.
 ISBN 978-1-4339-3906-8 (pbk.)
 ISBN 978-1-4339-3907-5 (6-pack)
 ISBN 978-1-4339-3905-1 (library binding)
 1. Polar bear–Juvenile literature. 2. Tundra animals–Juvenile literature. I. Title.
 QL737.C27S576 2011
 599.786–dc22

                                    2010000402

First Edition

Published in 2011 by
Gareth Stevens Publishing
111 East 14th Street, Suite 349
New York, NY 10003

Copyright © 2011 Gareth Stevens Publishing

Designer: Michael J. Flynn
Editor: Therese Shea

Photo credits: Cover, back cover, pp. 1, 5, 7, 9, 11, 15, 17, 21 Shutterstock.com;
p. 13 Paul J. Richards/AFP/Getty Images; p. 19 Paul Nicklen/National Geographic/
Getty Images.

Printed in the United States of America

CPSIA compliance information: Batch #CS10GS: For further information contact Gareth Stevens, New York, New York at 1-800-542-2595.

Table of Contents

Boldface words appear in the glossary.

Big Bear

Polar bears are the largest meat-eating animals on land. They live in the **tundra** around the **Arctic Ocean**. This is one of the coldest places on Earth.

A polar bear has a thick body, long neck, and short tail. Its small head has little, round ears. Some polar bears weigh 1,700 pounds (770 kg). That is as much as 10 people!

little ear

long neck

7

An Icy Tundra Life

Polar bears have fat that helps keep out the cold. They have fur that looks white, but it's really clear. The sun's rays shine through the fur and warm the bear's black skin.

clear fur

black skin

9

Polar bears have fur on the bottoms of their feet. This helps their feet stay warm when they walk. They have long claws that keep them from falling on ice and rocks. Their claws also help them hunt.

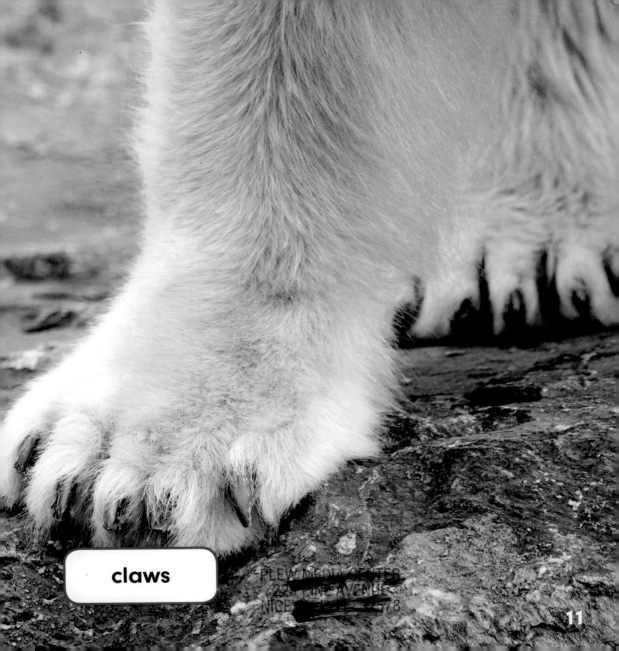

claws

Polar bears eat meat. They like to hunt seals. Polar bears wait near holes in the ice. When a seal comes up for air, the bear grabs it.

hole in ice

Polar bears are good swimmers. They use their front legs to push through the water. They catch seals under the water. Some even kill and eat small whales!

Polar bears find **mates** in the spring. Mothers have cubs during the winter. They take care of their cubs for several years. They find them food. They **protect** them from other polar bears, too.

cub

Polar Bear Hunters

No animals hunt polar bears. However, some people do. Arctic people use polar bear fur and meat. Some countries have laws against killing polar bears.

Disappearing Homes

Some people are worried that polar bears may die off. The ice in parts of the Arctic tundra is melting. Without their icy homes, how will polar bears live?

Fast Facts

Height	about 5 feet (1.5 meters) at the shoulder
Length	up to 10 feet (3 meters)
Weight	males: up to 1,700 pounds (770 kilograms) females: up to 650 pounds (300 kilograms)
Diet	mostly seals; also caribou, walrus, and small whales
Average life span	up to 30 years in the wild

Glossary

Arctic Ocean: the ocean around the North Pole

mate: one of a pair of animals that come together to make a baby

protect: to guard

tundra: flat, treeless plain with ground that is always frozen

For More Information

Books

Rosing, Norbert. *The World of the Polar Bear.* Richmond Hill, ON, Canada: Firefly Books, 2006.

Squire, Ann. *Polar Bears.* New York, NY: Children's Press, 2007.

Web Sites

National Geographic Kids: Polar Bears
kids.nationalgeographic.com/Animals/CreatureFeature/Polar-bear
Read facts and maps and see photos and videos of polar bears.

SeaWorld: Polar Bears
www.seaworld.org/infobooks/PolarBears/home.html
Read all kinds of information on polar bears, including more about their tundra homes.

Index

About the Author

Maeve T. Sisk is a writer and editor of several children's books. Her love of nature has led to a life of research and study of all things animal. She lives in New York City, where she often visits the polar bears at the zoo.

I LOVE TO TELL THE TRUTH

J'AIME DIRE LA VÉRITÉ

Shelley Admont

Illustrated by Sonal Goyal, Sumit Sakhuja

First edition, 2015
Traduit de l'anglais par Sophie Troff
Library and Archives Canada Cataloguing in Publication
I Love to Tell the Truth (French Bilingual Edition)/ Shelley Admont

ISBN: 978-1-77268-140-6 paperback
ISBN: 978-1-77268-139-0 eBook

Please note that the French and English versions of the story have been written to be as close as possible. However, in some cases they differ in order to accommodate nuances and fluidity of each language.

for those I love the most—S.A.

ceux que j'aime le plus —S.A.

It was a beautiful summer day. The sun was shining brightly. The birds were chirping. The butterflies and the bees were busy visiting the colorful flowers.

C'était une belle journée d'été. Le soleil brillait. Les oiseaux gazouillaient. Les papillons et les abeilles s'affairaient à butiner les fleurs de toutes les couleurs.

Little bunny Jimmy was playing ball in the backyard with his two older brothers. Their mom was watering her favorite daisies.

Jimmy le petit lapin jouait au ballon dans le jardin avec ses deux grands frères. Leur maman arrosait les marguerites, ses fleurs préférées.

"Be careful not to go near my flowers, boys," said mom.
– *Faites attention de ne pas jouer près de mes fleurs, les garçons, dit maman.*

"Sure mom," yelled Jimmy.
– *Bien sûr, maman, s'écria Jimmy.*

"I won't touch your daises mom," added the middle brother.
– *Je n'abîmerai pas tes marguerites, maman, ajouta son frère cadet.*

"Don't worry mom," said the oldest brother. "Your daisies are safe with us."
– *Ne t'inquiète pas, maman, dit l'aîné. Tes marguerites ne risquent rien avec nous.*

Mom went back to the house while the brothers continued to play outside, tossing the ball to each other.

Maman rentra dans la maison, tandis que les trois frères restèrent dehors, à jouer au ballon.

"Hey, let's play a different game now," said the oldest brother, twisting the ball.

– Et si on jouait à un autre jeu, proposa le frère aîné en faisant tournoyer le ballon.

"What game?" asked Jimmy.

– Quel jeu ? demanda Jimmy.

The oldest brother thought for a second. "Let's toss the ball in the air and see who gets to catch it first," he said.

Son grand frère réfléchit quelques secondes.
– Lançons le ballon en l'air et voyons qui le rattrape en premier.

"I like that," said Jimmy cheerfully.

– J'adore ! dit Jimmy avec enthousiasme.

"Let's start," cried the middle brother. "Throw the ball now."

– *C'est parti ! cria le frère cadet. Vas-y, lance le ballon.*

The oldest brother threw the ball up in the air as hard as he could.

Leur frère aîné lança le ballon en l'air de toutes ses forces.

All the bunnies looked up with their mouths open as the big orange ball quickly flew up. Soon, it began to fall back towards the ground.

Les trois lapins regardèrent, bouche bée, le gros ballon orange s'envoler à toute allure dans le ciel. Bientôt, il commença à redescendre.

Stretching out their hands, the brothers waited eagerly.

Bras écartés, les frères l'attendaient avec impatience.

When the ball was about to hit the ground, the older brothers ran to catch it.

Quand le ballon fut sur le point de toucher le sol, les deux plus grands coururent pour l'attraper.

In a flash, Jimmy leapt forward and reached the ball before them. "Hurray! I win!"

À la vitesse de l'éclair, Jimmy se jeta en avant et attrapa le ballon avant eux.
– Hourra ! J'ai gagné !

He jumped in joy and started to run around the backyard in excitement.

Il sauta de joie et se mit à faire le tour du jardin en courant, tout excité.

Suddenly, he tripped over a small rock and fell flat on the ground … right in the middle of his mom's favorite daisy plants.

Soudain, il trébucha sur une pierre et s'étala de tout son long... au beau milieu du massif de marguerites, les fleurs préférées de sa maman.

"Ouch!" yelled Jimmy, lifting his head out of the wet soil.

– Aïe ! hurla Jimmy, dont la tête avait tapé le sol humide.

His oldest brother ran over and helped him back to his feet. "Jimmy, are you hurt?" he asked.

Son frère aîné accourut pour l'aider à se remettre debout.
– Tu t'es fait mal, Jimmy ? demanda-t-il.

"No… I think I'm fine," said Jimmy.

– Non... Je crois que ça va, dit Jimmy.

"That's because these daisies are so soft, they protected you," explained his oldest brother.

– C'est parce que le lit de marguerites a amorti ta chute, expliqua son frère aîné.

All three bunnies looked sadly at their mom's favourite yellow flowers, which were now crushed. Some of them were broken.

Les trois lapins regardèrent d'un air triste les fleurs préférées de leur maman, qui étaient toutes écrasées. Certaines avaient leur tige cassée.

"Mom will not be happy to see this," murmured the oldest brother quietly.

– Maman ne va pas être contente de voir ça, murmura le frère aîné.

"That's for sure," agreed the middle brother.

– C'est sûr, admit le frère cadet.

"Please, please, don't tell mom that I did this. Pleeeeeaaaase…" begged Jimmy, slowly moving away from the ruined daisies.

– S'il vous plaît, s'il vous plaît, ne dites pas à maman ce que j'ai fait. S'il vous plaîîîît…. supplia Jimmy, en s'éloignant lentement du massif de marguerites en piteux état.

That moment, their mom came running out from the house. "Kids, what happened? I just heard someone scream. Are you all OK?"

À ce moment-là, leur maman sortit en courant de la maison.
– Que s'est-il passé les enfants ? J'ai entendu un cri. Tout le monde va bien ?

"We're fine, mom" said the oldest brother. "But your flowers..."

– On va bien, maman, dit le frère aîné. Mais tes fleurs...

It wasn't until that moment that their mom noticed the ruined flowerbed. She sighed. "How did this happen?" she asked, her shoulders drooping.

C'est alors que leur maman découvrit son massif de fleurs détruit. Elle soupira.
– Comment est-ce arrivé ? demanda-t-elle, les bras ballants.

"It was aliens," Jimmy hastened to answer. "They came from... out there..." He pointed to the sky. "Really, mom."
– *C'est des extraterrestres, se hâta de répondre Jimmy. Ils sont venus de... là-haut. Il pointa son doigt vers le ciel. C'est vrai, maman.*

Mom raised her eyebrow and looked into Jimmy's eyes. "Aliens?"
Maman fronça les sourcils et regarda Jimmy droit dans les yeux.
– *Des extraterrestres ?*

"Yes, and they flew away in their spaceship."
– *Oui, et après ils sont repartis dans leur vaisseau spatial.*

Mom sighed again. "It's good that they flew away," she said, "because now it's time for dinner. Don't forget to wash your hands. And Jimmy..."
Maman soupira de nouveau.
– *Heureusement qu'ils sont repartis, dit-elle, car c'est l'heure de manger. N'oubliez pas de laver vos mains. Et Jimmy...*

"Yes, mom," said Jimmy.
– *Oui maman, dit Jimmy.*

"Go wash your face too," she added.
– *Lave-toi la figure aussi, ajouta-t-elle.*

During the dinner, Jimmy was very quiet. He felt uncomfortable. He couldn't eat and he couldn't drink. He didn't even want to try his favourite carrot cake.

Pendant tout le dîner, Jimmy resta silencieux. Il était mal à l'aise. Il n'arrivait pas à manger ni à boire. Il ne voulut même pas prendre une part de gâteau aux carottes, son préféré.

At night, Jimmy couldn't sleep. Something didn't feel right. Getting up, he approached his oldest brother's bed.

Cette nuit-là, Jimmy n'arriva pas à dormir. Quelque chose le tourmentait. Il se leva et s'approcha du lit de son frère aîné.

"Hey, are you sleeping?" he whispered.

– Hé, tu dors ? chuchota-t-il.

"Jimmy, what happened?" mumbled his oldest brother, slowly opening his sleepy eyes. "Go back to your bed."

– Qu'est-ce qu'il y a, Jimmy ? marmonna son grand frère en entrouvrant ses paupières lourdes de sommeil. Retourne dans ton lit.

"I can't sleep. I keep thinking about mom's flowers," said Jimmy quietly. "I should have been careful with them."

– Je ne peux pas dormir. Je n'arrête pas de penser aux fleurs de maman, dit Jimmy tout bas. J'aurais dû faire attention à elles.

"Oh, that was an accident," said the oldest brother. "Don't worry. Go back to sleep!"

– *Oh, c'était un accident, dit son grand frère. Ne t'inquiète pas. Retourne te coucher !*

"But I should not have lied to mom," said Jimmy still staying there.

– *Mais je n'aurais pas dû mentir à maman, insista Jimmy, sans bouger d'un poil.*

The oldest brother sat up on his bed. "Yes," he agreed. "You should have told her the truth."

Le grand frère s'assit dans son lit.
– *Tu as raison, dit-il. Tu aurais dû lui dire la vérité.*

"I know," said Jimmy, shrugging his shoulders. "What am I going to do now?"

– *Je sais, dit Jimmy en haussant les épaules. Qu'est-ce que je vais faire maintenant ?*

"For now, go to sleep. And in the morning, you will tell mom the truth. Deal?"

– *Pour le moment, va te coucher. Et demain matin, tu diras la vérité à maman. D'accord ?*

"OK," said Jimmy and he trudged slowly to his bed.
– *D'accord, dit Jimmy, puis il retourna dans son lit en traînant les pieds.*

The next morning, he woke up very early, jumped out of his bed, and ran looking for his mom. She was in the backyard.

Le lendemain matin, il se réveilla tôt, sauta hors du lit et partit à la recherche de sa maman. Elle était dans le jardin.

"Mommy," Jimmy called. "I was the one who ruined your flowers, not the aliens." He ran over and hugged his mom.

– Maman, l'appela Jimmy. C'est moi qui ai abîmé tes fleurs, pas les extraterrestres.
Il courut vers elle et se jeta dans ses bras.

Mom hugged him back and replied, "I'm so happy that you told the truth. I know it wasn't easy, and I'm proud of you, Jimmy."

Maman le prit dans ses bras et dit :
– Je suis si contente que tu me dises la vérité. Je sais que ce n'est pas facile, et je suis fière de toi, Jimmy.

"Please don't be sad about the flowers. We'll think of something," said Jimmy.

– *Ne sois pas triste pour les fleurs. On va arranger ça, dit Jimmy.*

Mom shook her head. "I was not worried about the flowers. I was sad about you not telling me the truth."

Maman secoua la tête.
– *Je ne m'inquiétais pas pour les fleurs. J'étais triste que tu ne me dises pas la vérité.*

"I'm sorry, mom," said Jimmy. "I was sad also. I won't lie again."

– *Pardon, maman, dit Jimmy. J'étais triste aussi. Je ne mentirai plus jamais.*

After breakfast, Jimmy visited the local plant nursery with his dad. They bought some daisy seedlings and the whole family helped mom plant them.

Après le petit déjeuner, Jimmy accompagna son père chez le pépiniériste. Ils achetèrent des graines de marguerite et toute la famille aida maman à les planter.

Jimmy learned that telling the truth makes him and his family happy. That's why from that day on, he always tells the truth.

Jimmy en tira une précieuse leçon : dire la vérité avait rendu tout le monde heureux. C'est pourquoi, depuis ce jour, il dit toujours la vérité.

Let's Read About Insects
GRASSHOPPERS

by Susan Ashley

Reading consultant: Susan Nations, M.Ed., author/literacy coach/consultant

Please visit our web site at: www.earlyliteracy.cc
For a free color catalog describing Weekly Reader® Early Learning Library's
list of high-quality books, call 1-877-445-5824 (USA) or 1-800-387-3178 (Canada).
Weekly Reader® Early Learning Library's fax: (414) 336-0164.

Library of Congress Cataloging-in-Publication Data

Ashley, Susan.
    Grasshoppers / by Susan Ashley.
      p. cm. — (Let's read about insects)
    Summary: An introduction to the physical characteristics and behavior of the grasshopper.
    Includes bibliographical references and index.
    ISBN 0-8368-4054-2 (lib. bdg.)
    ISBN 0-8368-4061-5 (softcover)
    1. Grasshoppers—Juvenile literature. (1. Grasshoppers.) I. Title.
    QL508.A2A77   2004
    595.7'26—dc22   2003062180

This edition first published in 2004 by
Weekly Reader® Early Learning Library
330 West Olive Street, Suite 100
Milwaukee, WI 53212 USA

Copyright © 2004 by Weekly Reader® Early Learning Library

Editor: JoAnn Early Macken
Picture research: Diane Laska-Swanke
Art direction and page layout: Tammy Gruenewald

Picture credits: Cover, pp. 9, 19 © Brian Kenney; title © Gerald and Cynthia Merker/
Visuals Unlimited; pp. 5, 7, 17 © James P. Rowan; pp. 11, 13, 15 © Robert & Linda Mitchell;
p. 21 © Diane Laska-Swanke

Printed in the United States of America

1 2 3 4 5 6 7 8 9 08 07 06 05 04

Note to Educators and Parents

Reading is such an exciting adventure for young children! They are beginning to integrate their oral language skills with written language. To encourage children along the path to early literacy, books must be colorful, engaging, and interesting; they should invite the young reader to explore both the print and the pictures.

Let's Read About Insects is a new series designed to help children read about insect characteristics, life cycles, and communities. In each book, young readers will learn interesting facts about the featured insects and how they live.

Each book is specially designed to support the young reader in the reading process. The familiar topics are appealing to young children and invite them to read — and reread — again and again. The full-color photographs and enhanced text further support the student during the reading process.

In addition to serving as wonderful picture books in schools, libraries, homes, and other places where children learn to love reading, these books are specifically intended to be read within an instructional guided reading group. This small group setting allows beginning readers to work with a fluent adult model as they make meaning from the text. After children develop fluency with the text and content, the book can be read independently. Children and adults alike will find these books supportive, engaging, and fun!

— Susan Nations, M.Ed., author, literacy coach, and consultant in literacy development

Summer is the time
to see grasshoppers.
They often hop
through green fields.

Many grasshoppers are the same color as the grass. Their coloring helps them hide. They can be safe from their enemies. If they do not move, they might not be seen!

Grasshoppers have six legs. Their two back legs are much longer than their front legs. Their strong back legs help them jump. A grasshopper can jump twenty times its length!

Grasshoppers can also fly. They have four wings. The back wings are large. They do most of the work when a grasshopper flies. Some grasshoppers can fly very far.

In summer, grasshoppers look for a mate. Males attract females by singing. To sing, they rub their back legs on their front wings.

A female grasshopper digs a hole in the ground. She lays eggs in the hole. She covers them with a sticky material to protect them.

The eggs hatch.
Tiny grasshoppers
come out. The little
grasshoppers are
called **nymphs**.
They do not have
wings yet.

As their bodies grow, nymphs shed their skin. This process is called **molting**. Nymphs molt five or six times. Then they become adults.

Female grasshoppers lay their eggs in late summer. Most adults do not survive winter. In spring, their eggs hatch. A new life cycle begins.

Glossary

enemies — harmful or deadly things

fields — areas of open land with no trees or buildings

mate — a member of a breeding pair of animals

molting — shedding an outer layer of skin

nymphs — young insects that are not fully grown

For More Information

Books

Coleman, Graham. *Grasshoppers*. Milwaukee: Gareth Stevens, 1997.

Coughlan, Cheryl. *Grasshoppers*. Mankato, Minn.: Pebble Books, 2000.

Pascoe, Elaine. *Insects Grow and Change*. Milwaukee: Gareth Stevens, 2000.

Zuchora-Walske, Christine. *Leaping Grasshoppers*. Minneapolis: Lerner Publications, 2000.

Web Sites

Grasshoppers

www.ivyhall.district96.k12.il.us/4th/kkhp/insects/grasshopper.html
Grasshopper facts and photos

Index

About the Author

Susan Ashley has written over eighteen books for children, including two picture books about dogs, *Puppy Love* and *When I'm Happy, I Smile*. She enjoys animals and writing about them. Susan lives in Wisconsin with her husband and two frisky felines.